How to Homeschool College

Save Time, Reduce Stress, and Eliminate Debt

Lee Binz,
The HomeScholar

First Printing, 2019

Printed in the United States of America

Cover Design by Robin Montoya
Edited by Kimberly Charron

ISBN: 9781794628915

Disclaimer: Parents assume full responsibility for the education of their children in accordance with state law. College requirements vary, so make sure to check with the colleges about specific requirements for homeschoolers. We offer no guarantees, written or implied, that the use of our products and services will result in college admissions or scholarship awards.

How to Homeschool College

Save Time, Reduce Stress, and Eliminate Debt

What are Coffee Break Books?

How to Homeschool College is part of The HomeScholar's Coffee Break Book series.

Designed especially for parents who don't want to spend hours and hours reading a 400-page book on homeschooling high school, each book combines Lee's practical and friendly approach with detailed, but easy-to-digest information, perfect to read over a cup of coffee at your favorite coffee shop!

Never overwhelming, always accessible and manageable, each book in the series will give parents the tools they need to tackle the tasks of homeschooling high school, one warm sip at a time.

Everything about these Coffee Break Books is designed to connote simplicity, ease and comfort—from the size (fits in a purse), to the font and paragraph length (easy on the eyes), to the price (the same as a Starbucks Venti Triple Caramel Macchiato). Unlike a fancy coffee drink, however, these books are guilt-free pleasures you will want to enjoy again and again!

Table of Contents

Introduction

Why Homeschool College?

I know there are many frantic homeschoolers who are always busy with multiple tasks. Having kids makes it hard to keep it all together, much less keep your feet on the ground! The idea of homeschooling college may seem overwhelming or even impossible. Take heart! Homeschooling some or all of college is possible!

Focus on educating your child and don't disrupt everything merely because you want to get some college credits out of the way. Homeschool as usual and you will be in great shape to homeschool some college while your child is still in high school. You can translate the usual things into college credits later and you can even translate those credits into a college degree if they decide to attend.

If you have a freshman, a sophomore, or even a junior, you don't have to change everything you do to homeschool college. All you need to do is educate your child at their level in every subject all the time and everything will work out in the end.

Why Homeschool College?

First, homeschooling college can save money. We certainly noticed this. Classes are much cheaper at home.

Homeschooling a college class may cost about $200 per class. In contrast, a class at a regular college could be $400 per credit hour. Most college classes are three to five credits, so you're saving significant money by homeschooling college. Your child also spends less time at the university and less time can save you money. It saves many years of tuition, but also housing, room and board, and travel expenses.

Homeschooling college can help you guide gifted young students and nurture quality adults. You spend your life shaping and molding your child and you don’t want to give that all up and have a child with attitude. Instead, you can try to encourage good moral values as they grow into adulthood. By homeschooling college, you can continue to instill those values in your child.

Chapter 1

Benefits of Homeschooling College

Homeschooling college might not be for everyone, but for the student willing to put in the work, it can be an effective fast track to a college degree. Here are a few of the benefits of homeschooling college.

Provides outside documentation

Colleges like to see proof of learning from all students, not only homeschoolers. College level tests can provide this proof, like SAT scores do. Some colleges use these tests to award college credit. Others use the test to prove the student has some understanding of the subject but may not necessarily give college credit for it.

Outside documentation is a reflection of the child's education. I often tell people that their transcript grades should be reflected by their test scores in the same way a lake reflects the image of real objects. Test scores reflect your child's education. Even though we commonly think of this in terms of the SAT or ACT test used for college admission purposes, this is also true for subject tests used for homeschooling college. They still provide outside documentation that colleges like to see.

Allows your child to obtain college credit

Each university has its own unique policy. They vary widely, so check with the schools your child wants to attend. Some colleges accept specific CLEP scores, others accept them all, and some will not accept any. AP credits are also accepted at some colleges but not all. Some colleges accept community college credits but may not accept them all, or prefer community college credits but won't give college credit for community college courses.

At one of the colleges my sons applied to, they did not accept any CLEPs for credit but were thankful to have outside documentation of our students' grades. Another college accepted any CLEP with a score over 50 but would only accept up to one year of CLEP credits.

It's up to the parent and student to work together and figure out what their chosen colleges want. Each of the four colleges we applied to had a different policy. Consider your student, and what is most helpful for them. If push comes to shove, I suggest looking at your first choice college most closely. This is the college your child is most likely to go to should you decide not to homeschool college all the way through to a degree.

May allow your child to earn a college degree

You can mix and match the credits from different college level tests, combine them to meet college requirements, and fill in any additional credits from different sources to meet specific degree requirements. Then send these credits to a university that provides a diploma.

It's important to check the accreditation status of each university. Check the school's rules and regulations, and make sure they are still accredited by the time your child is done. At least this will give you a starting place. You don't want your child to use any university online because some are merely diploma mills. Unless it is an institution you know and trust, make sure it is accredited. Sometimes I recommend Lumerit Unbound as a resource because they are familiar with which universities are accredited and I trust their opinion.

Exceptions

Although homeschooling college can be helpful, it's not as useful for hands-on degrees. Classes such as science, technology, engineering, and medicine generally require on-campus work. Homeschooling college may not be helpful for kids who want to go to graduate school, either. An online degree may not transfer easily to a graduate school and your child might be unable to attend a medical school, law school, or other masters or doctorate programs. Some graduate programs care where your child earned an undergrad degree. Keep this in mind if grad school is part of your student's long-term plan.

Homeschooling college also requires student self-motivation. You cannot force a student to learn—the desire must come from within. This is probably three thousand times true when a child is eighteen and you can no longer tell them what to do! And especially true when they're working on a college degree and suddenly realize they are independent adults! As much as homeschooling requires self-motivation, homeschooling college requires an enormous amount of self-motivation.

I know that homeschooling college all the way through wouldn't have worked for either of my children. My older son was into science and engineering and wanted to get an engineering degree, which requires a certain amount of hands-on learning. Even though he took one year of community college and one year of homeschool college, he still had to attend university for four whole years to get his engineering degree. Homeschooling college didn't gain anything in time. However, we were thankful that the experiences helped him earn a full-tuition scholarship, so we could afford the four years of college.

My younger son wanted to pursue a law degree after earning a B.A. and had his heart set on going to Harvard. We knew that Harvard would not accept a homeschool college degree and the degree would have to come from a brick and mortar university.

Our children didn't earn a complete degree by homeschooling college. However, for both kids, homeschooling college was incredibly beneficial. It helped them get scholarships since it provided wonderful outside documentation. In theory, it could have shortened my youngest son's undergraduate degree, but he chose to go to school for four years because he loved it so much!

Chapter 2

Methods of Homeschooling College

One method of homeschooling college is to follow behind your student. This is where delight directed learning comes in. Have your child learn in their natural way, absorbing learning as they enjoy it, then try to find a college level test in the subject. Have them take a sample test at home to see whether they might be able to pass the subject test. The student then studies for the test to earn the best possible score and takes the test for real, after you're reasonably sure they will pass. Save and accumulate test scores to transfer them to a college or university later—one that will give college credit or a college degree.

Note that this process is repeated over and over. There are many subjects and tests to choose from. Your child takes a sample test at home to be sure they will pass the test before you have them take it for real.

Another method is to "Identify and Conquer." This is where you first figure out what kind of college credits your student needs and then you find a test in that subject. Use a textbook or create a class in that subject and study the course content. Instead of going to the beach and learning for fun, figure out what your student needs to know and encourage them to learn it on purpose.

Once you get to this point, it's the same strategy as following behind. Find a test in the subject, have the student take a sample test, study for the test using real sample tests, take the test for real in the testing environment, save and accumulate test scores, and then transfer them to the university or college. The key is to make sure your student will pass. There is a limit to how many times you can take some tests.

Which homeschooling college method will work for you and your child? There are a lot of moving parts, so think things through and sort out all the issues before deciding to pursue it.

Chapter 3

Collecting College Credit with CLEP

CLEP (College Level Examination) tests each cover one subject and there are a variety of specific subjects available. My son loves economics but there is no subject CLEP test simply on economics; instead, there is a test on microeconomics and a test on macroeconomics. These are detailed, college-level tests. There are 33 subject areas and over 2900 colleges award credit for these tests.

Scores

The score range for most CLEP tests is from 20 to 80, as determined by the College Board. The average score of an

SAT is 500 and the average score on a CLEP test is 50. A score of 50 is roughly equivalent to getting 50 percent correct on a sample test. When your student takes a sample test at home, make sure they will score well above 50 percent before taking the test for real.

Every college has a different idea of what is an acceptable score for college credit. The College Board suggests that any score over 50 be awarded college credit but colleges aren't required to do so. Some colleges require a score of 60 or above on one test but 50 or above on another test. Their requirements are non-negotiable!

CLEP tests are computer-based. The student is given a set amount of time to complete the test. These tests are available year-round, every day of the week, every week of the year. If your student gets a hankering to study economics and take the CLEP test, they can easily do so within a year.

Notification of the score is received immediately after the test. Before the test, the test taker must decide where they want to send the scores, or not to send the scores anywhere right now and simply receive the score report as they walk out the building. Scores are collected on a transcript that looks much like a college transcript. Colleges get their own copy directly from the College Board. By seeing the transcript, I knew exactly what the course title should be on my child's high school transcript (since my kids were taking CLEPs during their high school years) and exactly what their scores should be.

When we homeschooled college, I knew my children would do quite well on CLEP tests. I knew that our first choice college accepted CLEP tests, so I chose to have their scores reported immediately to their number one college. We didn't do the same for other chosen colleges—I waited and let those test scores accumulate to send directly to other colleges together. It's more expensive, about $5 to $10 per class, to wait and learn the scores are before sending them. But it seemed reasonable at the time.

CLEP Resources

For a general assessment, to figure out whether your student can pass a CLEP test, use the CLEP Official Study Guide. It provides one sample test in every subject area. It's just a quick assessment, a pretest if you will, to determine if they can pass.

I gave my children the CLEP study guide and showed them the names on each test in the table of contents. I told them they could take any test they were interested in. Then they took a sample test to see if they could pass. Once I knew they could come close to passing, we studied in-depth using the specific subject test study guide.

I recommend the REA Study Guides.

Each one is for an individual test and includes full-length practice tests. Some include online preparation as well, so your student can take the test on the computer like the real test.

My son Alex knew he would need to take Psychology at some point in college and he didn't want to. It was clear that he could not pass a CLEP test yet when he took a sample test and his score was low. Then we got the study guide for psychology and he read it cover-to-cover. He too more practice tests and eventually was confident that he would pass. He took the test, passed it, and didn't have to take a psychology course in college.

Chapter 4

College Credit with AP

The AP (Advanced Placement) tests are also available from the College Board and are also taken one subject at a time. What makes AP test unique is that they are the most common credit by exam taken by high school students. High school students are familiar with AP tests and less familiar with CLEPs since they're usually taken by adult learners.

The AP is offered in over 30 subject areas and they do add subjects from time to time. AP exams are offered both at public and private schools and there is an option to include homeschoolers. Look around for a school that allows homeschoolers.

AP Exam

AP exams are quite long. They include long essays, short essays, and a few multiple-choice questions. Scores range from one to five—a much narrower range than most exams. These scores can be tied directly to a college grade. For many colleges, a perfect score of five means that they will award the student an *A*. A score of four is a *B*, and a three is a *C*. Three is the lowest possible grade to get credit for and there's a small margin of error. AP exams are offered each May.

One of my young homeschool friends was quite gifted in language arts and took an AP exam because she wanted one under her belt. She took American Literature and said she knew for a fact that she would get a perfect five but had a bad day and earned a four! The AP score of four was automatically transferred to the college she applied to, as a letter grade of *B*, which was the only *B* she received during her entire college education! In every other class she received *A, A+*, or *A-*.

This is why I keep harping on the importance of making sure your child will pass the test! Your child could have a bad day. If you think they will get a five and they have a bad day and get a four, that is not the worst thing that could happen. If they take a test thinking that they will be lucky to get a three and have a really bad day and don't pass, it will be on their permanent record.

The AP questions are long and use challenging wording. When I looked over the AP exam and study guide to see whether it would be a good fit for my children, I was a little surprised because it included interpreting political cartoons from the 1800s. That frustrated me, and I don't know how my children dealt with it; I couldn't imagine how interpreting a 100-year-old cartoon would be a useful skill in the long run.

There's a difference between AP exams and AP classes. An AP class designation requires approval from the College Board. You submit your plan and course outline to the College Board to approve; if you get approval, then you can state "AP Class" on your child's transcript.

However, even if your child doesn't take an AP class, they can still take an AP test. The class has a curriculum, but your child can learn the material on their own, sign up for an AP test, and take it. If your student follows this route, instead of putting AP on their transcript, you can include "Honors" instead. You might write "Honors Microeconomics" instead of AP Microeconomics.

There are many study materials available. Because I did not give AP classes or exams to my own students, I can't specifically recommend one over the other.

Chapter 5

College Credit with DSST

DSST exams (formerly known as DANTES Subject Standardized Tests) originated from the DANTES exams offered to military personnel. There are over 30 exams available, including math, social sciences, business, physical sciences, applied technology, and the humanities. DSST exams cost about the same as AP and CLEP exams.

These exams are recognized and recommended by thousands of colleges. Your student can take them year-round at colleges, universities, businesses across the U.S., and in various countries. DSST exams are taken by high school students, homeschool students, college students, adult learners, the military, and veterans.

DSST exams are a type of Prior Learning Assessment—a way for students to earn college credit using information that they've gained through self-study, one test at a time. Your student doesn't necessarily have to take a class—simply do some self-study. If they're able to pass the test, then they can get college credit.

Each DSST exam has a different credit value. Your student can certainly earn part of a college degree but would need other tests, such as CLEP, AP or online classes to pull it all together into a college degree. The website has a great mentoring program, so your student may or may not need additional support beyond what you receive when you pay for the test.

Keys to Success

Regardless of which test option you choose for your child, they will need photo ID, no matter how young they are. Cheating has been happening for hundreds of years, so schools are strict about requiring identification from every student.

Institutions may also require your child to enter the testing site as a student. My kids took CLEP exams at a vocational technical college, and we had to register them as students of the college. They each received a student ID number and we had to pay a fee for them to become registered students, even though they were only signed up as auditing students. They also had to pay for each test.

The most important key to success is to make sure your student will pass the test. Pre-test with the knowledge that they will pass and use a study guide.

Have them take the test for real once you're certain they will pass.

Chapter 6

Distance Learning

Online college, or what we call homeschooling college, is not a new phenomenon at all. Distance learning used to mean students mailing their tests and assignments to teachers and waiting for the teachers to grade them and send them back. Now, distance learning is much faster because everything is done online.

Books I recommend for distance learning include:

- *Accelerated Distance Learning*
- *Bear's Guide to Earning Degrees* by Distance Learning

Lumerit Unbound

You can homeschool college at home independently, but there are times when it's worth it to have a mentor. I recommend Lumerit Unbound (getunbound.org) to help students homeschool college, because they are trustworthy. They can be your child's mentors and help think through the issues, find out which tests to collect to get a specific degree, figure out how to transfer credits, and determine whether they can be transferred. Lumerit Unbound provides helpful guidance, especially if your student is looking for a complete degree such as a bachelor's degree in business administration.

For Lumerit Unbound, you do pay a coaching fee. You also need to buy books for the test materials, pay test fees and enrolment for the college where your student takes the tests, and pay enrolment for the college where the degree is accumulated plus course fees.

To get a degree, it might cost $13,000 to $16,000.

Using Lumerit Unbound to homeschool college is not free. It still costs a lot of money, but it doesn't cost quite as much as traditional college.

College Suggestions

Thomas Edison State College

The first college I suggest for distance learning is Thomas Edison State College since they offer online degrees. This college is often used by Lumerit Unbound. They have a flexible policy. Their website states they will accept credits from other institutions, provided that the institutions are regionally accredited. Your child will be able to combine community college and other credits into a degree.

Thomas Edison gives a full evaluation of your student's credits when they apply. If your child already has CLEP scores,

AP scores, or has taken community college courses, it can all be evaluated upon application. Then, you'll know how many more tests are needed to complete the degree.

Regent University

Regent University has an online peer mentorship program. The tuition is the same, whether your child attends on campus or whether they take classes online. I'm familiar with Regent University since my niece graduated from their law school.

They offer a Bachelor of Arts (BA) and Associate of Arts (AA). Their BA is a four-year degree and the AA is a two-year degree. A Christian ministry degree is also available. If your child is too young to go to a Bible college and is interested in Christian ministry, homeschooling college is a way for them to get that sort of degree.

Western Governor's University

Western Governor's University is a public university—not Christian, not private, but it is nationally known. It's online, accelerated, and accredited. They require students to be at least sixteen years old. For a public university, that's generous, because they're usually not that flexible.

Other states also have schools like WGU, and they work together to promote each other. This is an option for families who are interested in homeschooling college but are looking for a more secular university education.

Chapter 7

Community College

When I speak to groups, I sometimes express my dissatisfaction with community college. Extremely popular with homeschoolers, I often get asked why I am hesitant about the current trend. In my own experience, and in talking with other parents, I have determined that community college can be a *Rated-R* environment. Even with careful control of the curriculum and selection of the teachers, the college environment is still an adult situation.

Professors at these schools have told me they use the *sex sells* approach. In a high school, although there are many issues, there are generally limits to the use of inappropriate material to sell their educational product. There are no such limits in a community college. They cater to the broad expanse of adults, not the unique subset of homeschooled young adults who don't want to mix education with unrelated material.

Community college provides the socialization you normally see in a public high school. Because they are public institutions, community colleges come complete with the public school worldview and academics, which is often the reason many homeschoolers avoid public school in the first place.

I know that I have a unique perspective on community college and I don't think for a minute that my view is right, and others are wrong. Community college is a current fad in homeschooling, and my job is to provide information. Armed with this knowledge, you can avoid the lemming mentality and make choices with your eyes wide open. Parents are the best people to make these choices. I see parents feeling pressured to put their children into dual enrollment during high school. I'm trying to remove that pressure, so they can make judgments based on their understanding, and not merely because others are doing it.

Our Community College Stories

My children attended community college during their last year before university. These are our experiences with a local community college:

- The student bookstore sold pornographic magazines next to the engineering textbooks.
- The calculus professor dropped the f-bomb in every sentence. One of the physics professors used sexual positions to describe physics principles. As luck would have it, our children were assigned to a different professor.

- The "Music Improvisation" class book stated, "I capitalize the word 'Self' because I was taught to capitalize the name of God, and only God can create music." The class included a mantra each day, "I am Good, I am Great, I am God." We declined to enroll our children in that class.
- The French teacher showed movies with unclothed people to demonstrate the culture.
- The speech teacher and the curriculum were great, but one of the other students presented a speech on the religion of sex that was eye-opening.
- The political science class was taught by a self-proclaimed Marxist.
- Within the first two weeks of community college, my children had completed all the reading and assignments they could and spent the

remaining six weeks learning how to do nothing and get *A's* without trying.

- Not many classes would challenge my sons and at the same time not offend our faith. My political science aficionado ended up taking only engineering science and math classes. I'm certainly glad he was able to tolerate differential equations!

- On the bright side, the community college did offer an honors program, with additional coursework. This seemed to help the academic level slightly, but still did not bring it up to the difficulty level of our homeschool.

- For the first time, my children encountered people who didn't want to learn. Some students felt that a 0.7 GPA was a passing grade and that receiving a 2.0 in a class was *good.* Many students didn't show up for class or didn't participate in classroom discussion even when they knew the answers.

Stories from Another Parent

My daughter just started attending the local community college this week. Already she has an assignment from her Art Appreciation professor that has me wondering what colleges are teaching these days. *rolling eyes* A piece of paper was passed around the class with a list of two items to compare. They were to choose one set and are to write a paper. My daughter saw the word "chapel" and picked it, although she didn't know what the other word was.

We now know that it's a series of "art" (cough-cough) films called the *Cremaster Cycle*. She and I have seen the trailer, and both of us have found it to be offensive. The artist based his work on a specific muscle

> of the male anatomy, and the whole movie is bizarre representations of the reproductive systems. Plus, there are some gruesome death scenes too. We saw all this during just the five-minute trailer!
>
> She's said that she's going to talk with her professor about picking a different group to compare. I pray that the teacher is understanding and won't give my daughter a hard time. I know that "art" is subjective, but SHEESH!
>
> ~ Jen in Texas

Jen was extremely surprised that this could happen at a community college in her area because they live in the middle of the conservative Bible Belt.

Being forewarned is not enough. Linda heard me speak at a college fair and was aware of the risks. Last fall she sent me this note:

> Two weeks into our 16-year-old daughter's first quarter at community college, two pornographic reading assignments were handed out in her required English class. I knew from prior discussions with you that dual enrollment was risky. However, I thought that if we were selective in the classes we took, we could avoid the problems you had warned me about. We are looking for alternatives at this time.
>
> ~Linda in Washington

Now her daughter is faced with a permanent academic record that may include a withdrawal or failing grade, and they are considering their next steps.

It's not Naiveté

I do not believe that this kind of experience at community college is only a problem for young students and I don't believe it has anything to do with naiveté in general. Read this mother's blog post:

> Now the bad news. There are no morals, no discipline, and evolution and political correctness reign supreme. The students in the classes were very disrespectful. I could not believe how much they mouthed off to the teachers. In my algebra class, students would say, "I hate your teaching, you are the worst teacher."
>
> In speech class, one student offered to pay for the exam ahead of time. Cheating was rampant. If you want to pass without studying, I suppose it's possible. Students were programming answers in their calculators, getting up to "go to the bathroom" during the exams, and the math teacher even left the classroom while we were taking an exam!

As far as sending your kids to these colleges, all I can say is that you better be sure that your child is real grounded in the Word. That they have more than a head knowledge of God and that they are determined to live by His principles. If not, you are sending your child into a war zone without weapons. It was bad in my day (1960s) but today, it's unbelievably worse. In the 60s, at least there were some morals left. Today, there are none.

I was talking with one little girl who was programming her calculator with answers to the Algebra quiz. She offered to program mine since I didn't know how to do it. When I said that I couldn't sleep at night if I did that, she answered very sincerely, "It's not really cheating. I'm only taking this course because it's required. It's different if it's your major." She was sincere in her answer and believed that that was OK!

~ Cindy Downes' blog post, "My First Exposé of College"

Cindy is neither a young student, nor is she naive, yet she had issues and unique difficulties. The stories we hear about homeschoolers going to college are the same stories we would hear if our adult friends were attending college. It's not the children, it's the environment.

Another mother reported that her local Christian college does not accept community college writing courses. They believe that community college English courses involve topics that are much too controversial for high school students. This university has responded to the community college environment by rejecting all such college credits. Although this is unusual, it's best to check with the university your child hopes to attend, so you aren't disappointed.

Community college mixes the best and brightest students with those who struggle the most in the same class. The Florida Department of Education (fldoe.org) website explains:

> Our Honors and Early College/Dual Enrollment programs attract some of the best and brightest minds. Our open-door policies allow students who need remediation to get the skills they need for college-level courses.

Two such varied situations—two sentences side by side—representing two students sitting next to each other in class. It can be difficult for either child in this situation.

Public universities often (but not always) have higher academic expectations and the student population often has higher academic expectations. Community college students are frequently at a remedial level in one way or another. The students are often not ready for a university–financially, academically, or socially. This means they can be a challenge to educate, making it a unique educational setting.

I asked my son if he thought community college had been a mistake. At the age of 20 he said, "Yes!" If I could do it over again, I would not have let them engage in dual enrollment. I would have either continued homeschooling and achieved outside documentation through testing or graduated them a year early and sent them to a Christian university, where the cultural and academic clash would have been less severe.

Is Community College Right for Your Family?

Ask your local friends about their community college experience. They may start with the positives, "We had a wonderful experience but . . ." Listen for the *but.* If you heard this disclaimer about a public high school, would you be tempted to enroll your child?

Think deeply about your feelings on public and secular universities. If you would not want your child to go to a public university or if you are concerned about the values at a private university, then community college will not be a good fit. One parent enrolled her children in community college and then explained, "My husband and I think that college is not worth the money and what kids are taught in college is questionable. If they choose to go to college, the school will be carefully chosen." Consider that if a university is not a good fit for moral or religious reasons, a community college is unlikely to fit your family, either.

I attend many college fairs. One community college representative took me aside and said, "Please tell homeschoolers not to send their children to community college! We have adjudicated people in the classes!" She said that felons and registered offenders were known to be on campus, and she worried about innocent homeschoolers. I'm sure the criminal element is relatively rare (although how would we know?) but the point is still important.

If you choose to send your child, there are some strategies that may mitigate trouble. Find a support group of like-minded individuals, either homeschoolers or Christian groups that meet regularly. Utilize the buddy system and keep your kids in class with another homeschooler. Carefully read all online comments about the professor at RateMyProfessor.com. Preview the textbooks before the first day of class.

When you are considering community college, don't view it through rose-colored glasses as if it's a perfect educational utopia. Keep your eyes open to the fact that it may be more *Rated-R* than your student is ready for. If the crowd seems to follow the community college route, that doesn't mean you have to follow along. Consider carefully, know your child, and trust your own judgment.

Chapter 8

Incorporating College Credits on a Homeschool Transcript

After collecting college credits, you need to incorporate them on your child's homeschool transcript. Remember that high school credits are measured differently than college credits. If you have one standard credit by exam, either a CLEP or an AP test, it's usually equivalent to three or six college credits, but it's only equivalent to one high school credit.

When your child takes a test, it demonstrates a college level amount of knowledge in that subject. An entire college level class is usually earned in three months. A class with that amount of material usually takes a student a whole year to learn, which is why three or six credits is equivalent to one high school credit—it goes faster when you're in college and it's measured differently.

The name of the CLEP or AP test your student takes can be the same on their homeschool transcript. When it comes to naming the class, you don't have to do a lot of thinking.

If they pass a college level class, then you know your student would do well on an equivalent high school test in the same subject area, because college information is more advanced than high school information. If they pass a college class, I recommend giving your student an *A* for the high school level equivalent. Because it is a college level class, I recommend including "Honors" in the course title. If a college asks whether it's a regular class or an honors class, it is definitely an honors level class.

Don't do any double-dipping when you incorporate information in the transcript. If you use a curriculum to study microeconomics and then your child takes the microeconomics test, they don't get two high school credits in microeconomics. You can only count the studying and the test once.

Careful Credits

Look carefully at your child's credits. One way to signify where credits came from on the transcript is to create an acronym for each source. Include "CLEP" next to the class name for every CLEP test, for instance. Whatever it is, use the appropriate acronym before the class title to show your student took classes at that specific institution or through that test.

Cost Comparison

There is a cost per college credit and a cost to obtain the entire college degree, but you need to balance this by considering college debt and your ability to pay it back. If you thought homeschooling college was expensive, wait until you buy college level books—they're so much more expensive! One of the benefits of homeschooling college is that you can pay as you go. Each time you have enough money to buy a book, you can buy the book and have your child take the test. Instead of a huge, four-year commitment and taking out a loan for $30,000, you can pay as you go.

If you are thinking about homeschooling college strictly because of college debt, weigh the pros and cons. When you are a homeschooler, you are used to an expense for the cost of education. When those expenses continue into the college years, it's not much different—you're still paying for their education. You have money that is used for education and you can use these dollars for college education as well. It may be more expensive than simply homeschooling because your student is at the college level, but it may be worth it to you.

I usually encourage parents to think about the ability to pay back any debt that may be incurred. If the child were to live at home after college graduation and get a minimum wage job, how much could they pay back in one year? For one year, you could put up with almost anything, even a messy young person coming back to live with you. If they could pay back $15,000 to $20,000 by working for minimum wage, it might be a reasonable amount of debt to take on. By going to that worse-case scenario, you have some assurance they'll be able to pay it back and get out of debt quickly.

Many of the college students I know who incurred some college debt have been able to pay it back by being conscientious with their money. I don't think you need to homeschool college for the sake of not having any debt, but it's something to think about.

There are more things to consider beyond college debt. If your student is immature and you're relatively confident they might fall apart or fall into the wrong crowd by attending a brick and mortar school, homeschooling college might make more sense. There's also the social and emotional cost of sending a student that may be too young for college level material. If they have issues they struggle with, the emotional costs may be too high and homeschooling college may be the best choice.

Remember that the cost of homeschooling college is not inexpensive, but it's less expensive than the traditional four-year institution. Consider what's best for your student and research the possibilities before you make any decisions.

Appendix 1

Open College Courseware for Homeschooling College

Cosmo Learning

Provides video lectures, courses, documentaries, books, quizzes, lecture notes, open courseware and much more.

Khan Academy

Providing more than 3,200 free educational videos to anyone anywhere.

MIT Open CourseWare

The most popular open course program across the world. Some courses offer videos along with printable materials.

MIT World

Features videos of the most recent speakers and guests from across the campus and around the world.

Project Gutenberg

A free online library of public domain literature, Project Gutenberg offers over 33,000 free eBooks to read online and download.

Internet Archive

A non-profit digital library offering free universal access to books, movies & music, as well as 150 billion archived web pages.

Open Yale Courses

Free access to introductory courses taught by professors and scholars at Yale University.

Appendix 2

College for Struggling Learners

Dealing with learning challenges is difficult, but in high school it can become seriously concerning. You don't have to be afraid! With the great student-to-teacher ratio of homeschooling, and the love for your child, you can overcome learning struggles! A parent is a successful homeschooler if their child is performing to the best of their ability. It's an emotional struggle, best understood by other parents who have faced the challenge.

Homeschooling works because it can improve children's academic performance level, even allowing them to achieve grade level in their most challenging subjects. Younger children thrive at home, without teachers labeling them or children teasing them. Parents can use a learning style that works for each child and keep the repetitive work to the minimum their child needs to practice and learn. Older children can still learn high school subjects without relying on their weakest abilities to get the information. If reading is a challenge your child can learn through listening, if writing is difficult your child can answer questions orally. Without being slowed down by their unique learning challenges, teens can progress through all the grade levels and into successful adulthood.

Debbie was at her lowest point when she realized her 12-year-old son, Dan, could not read or write in his Sunday school classes. She had to carefully shield him from others' judgment. Her homeschool friends were understanding but she worked hard to keep him away from situations in which he would have to read aloud. She was distraught.

They changed curriculum repeatedly, hoping each time that a new curriculum would change everything. It seemed like nothing would ever work. He struggled with learning all the way through high school. She never had him officially tested because she didn't want him to be labeled as an adult.

Dan has achieved wonderful things since graduating homeschool! When Dan turned 18, he started working at Starbucks. An excellent worker, he received nothing but positive feedback, which motivated him to continue his education and decided to attend college. He didn't score well on the SAT, so they did not report his scores to colleges. He entered college "through the back door" his mother said, by attending community college first. His excellent work ethic and love of learning helped him thrive where others felt adrift.

Dan transferred from community college to the university with a 3.89 grade point average. There were 300 applicants to the business school that year and Dan was one of only 100 admitted. Debbie says, "He finally realizes he can do it!"

Debbie has some great advice for parents. “Don't push [your child] before they are ready.” She was glad she kept him home, so he could avoid the negative feedback from a public school setting. Debbie read aloud to Dan constantly—even reading his high school textbooks, when necessary. Verbal assessments were used in all his classes and essay writing was introduced much later than usual.

She recommends books by Dr. Raymond Moore, including *Better Late Than Early: A New Approach to Your Child's Education*, and Grace Llewellyn’s *The Teenage Liberation Handbook: How to Quit School and Get a Real Life and*

Education, and Cynthia Tobias' *The Way They Learn*. She says, "You feel like you're failing—like you didn't do something right." Don't be deterred, though. It takes a lot of one-on-one time, but that's the benefit of homeschooling. Read textbooks and the classics to your child. Even in college, they can be allowed help with reading.

In her lowest moments, Debbie would remember her grandfather. He also could not read. His wife read blueprints to him each night, so he would be prepared for work the next day. Still, her grandfather was a successful businessman. He was able to compensate. Her son Dan can more than compensate now.

Teenagers Change Their Minds

Debbie's biggest surprise was realizing that Dan wanted a college degree. She never thought he would go to college and only vaguely considered a technical school. But when he worked at Starbucks, he identified his gift in business. Her additional advice is the same as mine. She says, "Even if you think they won't go to college, they may, so always be prepared!"

Dan is so thankful he was homeschooled. He says he would never put his own children in public school. He knows that if he hadn't been homeschooled, he wouldn't be where he is today. Nurturing is critical, and homeschooling can provide that best. Debbie says, "I remember the hopelessness. They **can** succeed and excel—just give them the tools."

Learning to Teach

JoAnn homeschooled her two daughters, feeling extremely unsure of her abilities, until they were officially diagnosed with learning disabilities. Once she had the diagnosis, JoAnn realized homeschooling was the best option. She didn't want her girls ostracized and placed in a *special* group that would have a negative effect on their socialization skills. Even her mother became increasingly supportive of homeschooling after the diagnosis.

Her two girls could not read until half-way through 5th grade. They struggled in reading, writing, and spelling. JoAnn took her children to The Slingerland Institute (slingerland.org). She recommends two pamphlets that really helped her cope, “Why Wait for a Criterion of Failure” and “An Adaptation of the Orton-Gillingham Approach for Classroom Teaching of Reading,” both by Beth Slingerland.

JoAnn's advice is "Never despair! The timing of brain growth is on your **child’s** timetable, not yours. Accept it, because you certainly can't change it!" She wishes she would have dropped more academic subjects when they were in elementary school. Still, she is so glad she homeschooled. Homeschooling is better for dyslexic kids for the positive encouragement and socialization."

She taught with multi-sensory input and multi-sensory output. In every subject, she worked to provide lessons with audio, visual, **and** tactile input. She would supplement courses with drama, hands-on projects, and verbal assessments all the way through school. Her daughters were especially helped by using color. Her daughter still color codes her college lecture notes to improve retention.

JoAnn's eldest daughter went directly into a university and majored in biology with a minor in chemistry. She recently graduated with an advanced degree and is a Veterinarian Technician. Her younger daughter also went directly into a university. She will graduate with a degree in interior design and has already done some design work for Bill Gates as a college intern. Both girls were successful in college.

Learning to Cope When Children are Young

Jill is hesitant about labeling her daughter in any way, but knew she faced unique challenges even though she wasn't formally diagnosed. Her daughter recently became a National Merit Scholarship Semi-Finalist. Here is what Jill says about her daughter's struggles:

> She worked hard and I'm very proud of her. She is the daughter that would fit into the statement, "I could never homeschool my child because . . ." She is very active, intense, dramatic and a joy to be around. I am convinced that if she were in the public school, we would have been **encouraged** to put her on medications (the standard line around here, when she is getting jumpy is to "run up to the mailbox

> and get the mail" which is a mile round trip). She has forced me to think outside of the box and, well, it is an adventure I'm sorry to see come to a close.

Like the other mothers, Jill was able to find a way to harness strengths and weaknesses and teach her child to compensate for difficulties. With a parent's close attention, unique coping mechanisms can develop. A homeschool parent can see small successes and learn to instill new ways of coping into their child with each challenge.

Joelle is right in the thick of things with her young child. I asked her for some advice for others, and she emphasizes that coping comes from faith. This is Joelle's experienced advice.

> A learning *disability* (a word I hesitate to use for anyone who doesn't have a severe condition) isn't something you can just make go

away if you have a clinic and a handful of web links. A learning challenge is best addressed by being sensitive to learning style and interests, which, as you know, vary from child to child.

A learning challenge is also a mindset, a lifestyle, and sore knees from prayer. A learning challenge means you'll come face-to-face with your pessimism and lack of faith through tears of mourning for the child you don't have. But lest anyone abandon hope, a learning challenge also means seeing God answer those tears by turning them to tears of what is, hands down, absolutely the most incredible joy when you see the triumphs. You will see those victories sooner or later on Earth or in Heaven.

A learning challenge leads to personal growth in the siblings of the challenged child. A learning challenge is a worldview, a lens, a perspective. It's the fierce mother-bear love you have when you whisper to your child, "Don't listen to the naysayers. I love you no matter what, and I'm still your teacher."

I can offer a short list of helpful resources, but there is only one resource on here that I can guarantee hands down will help everyone. The rest can be labeled of interest.

1. *The Bible* Children are people—in fact, they are the most human of people. There are lots of passages on how we are to deal with our fellow humans. This is the only resource on this list that I can guarantee will help.

2. *Last Child in the Woods: Saving Our Children From Nature-Deficit Disorder* by Richard Louv—read this concurrently with #3

3. *Smart Moves: Why Learning Is Not All in Your Head* by Carla Hannaford - which will probably lead to curiosity about #4

4. *Brain Gym: Simple Activities for Whole Brain Learning* or similar therapies

5. The National Association for Child Development (nacd.org)

While your children are young, find what works for your child. Do your research, beginning with the Learning Disabilities Association, ldaamerica.org. As your child grows, there is a shift in your purpose. Eventually, your purpose becomes learning how to compensate for challenges to allow your child to succeed in college and career.

Learning to Compensate with Older Teens

In a school setting, children are often given an accommodation for their learning challenges. In the adult world, people learn to compensate for their weaknesses all the time. If your child struggles with writing, you can help them learn to compensate.

Teach keyboarding skills with Mavis Beacon Teaches Typing. Provide audio books to increase vocabulary when your child can't read advanced books. While parents of young children rely on audio books for literature, and you can find high school curriculum and textbooks with an audio download available. Even popular science texts sometimes offer inexpensive audio book versions. Although not perfect, it's also possible to have a computer read aloud texts and websites.

Consider investing in adaptive technology that will help your teen compensate. One popular example is Dragon Naturally Speaking, a speech-recognition software that types for your child. It gives "users the power to create documents, reports and emails three times faster than most people type—with up to 99 percent accuracy." My husband tried the software and had a lot of fun with it. For a computer-savvy teen, it should be a breeze to use. Your teen will have to "train" the computer to understand their voice. Once the computer types what they say, some editing may be required, but it's much less work.

I do think Dragon Naturally Speaking can help improve academic performance across many subjects, allowing your child to perform at a high school level. They can use it to compose reports or assignments in all their subjects quickly. Then they can succeed in history, economics, and science without being penalized for their weaknesses in English. This can improve their love of learning, and lead to a better educated child in the long run.

Seek a diagnosis and accommodation when it will help your child. If you think a diagnosis will help **you** teach your child, then it will help your child. It you think a diagnosis will help your child get into college or succeed in college, then it will help your child. In this situation, testing will be worthwhile, even if it's inconvenient.

Learning to Succeed in College

Keep in mind your long-terms goals. You want your child to grow up, have their own home, and succeed and thrive in anything they choose, whether it's college or career.

Some colleges specialize in learning disabilities and you can see them proudly sharing their specialization when attending a college fair. Many colleges offer support services to help students with learning challenges.

Anita in Missouri writes:

> All of the colleges we visited with my son had learning help centers that provided free assistance in many areas: studying, writing, test prep, and many other areas as well.

You are not alone; there is support for your child in college. Some colleges understand and accept any learning issues without hesitation.

Find helpful colleges by attending a college fair. You can do additional research with this college guide that prioritizes specialized college searches, *The K&W Guide to Colleges for Students with Learning Differences*.

It's helpful to prepare for the SAT or ACT when possible. High schoolers face multiple timed tests in their life, but below average scores are a recipe for failure and negative feedback. Instead, request accommodation for the SAT and ACT if necessary, which does require a doctor's diagnosis.

If you don't want accommodation for college admission tests, a diagnosis may not be necessary. You may feel comfortable with your homeschooling methods and don't need additional help or direction. A specialist may not have an impact on what you're doing and a diagnosis may not change anything or be worth the cost. On the other hand, if you are completely baffled about how to teach your student and the input of a specialist will help you, then evaluation may be useful.

Ten Tips for Handling the College Admission Process

Colleges love diversity, to encourage vibrant interaction in classroom discussions. They are looking for all different kinds of personal experiences and backgrounds. Because your child's struggles are part of who they are, they can bring much-needed perspective to college!

1. **Start thinking early.** Create a plan for maximum flexibility for your child, to be prepared for any college or career choice.

2. **Take college prep classes.** Use accommodations and any learning styles or methods that work.

3. **Be creative with curriculum.** Use outside the box subjects and curriculum. For example, teach ASL for foreign language.

4. **Encourage confidence and assertiveness.** Teens should understand their medications and what they need.

5. **Find adaptive technology.** Determine what will help them

succeed. For example, consider using Dragon Naturally Speaking.

6. **Document disability when helpful.** Obtain a recent diagnosis and assessment, when you think it will help your child. Then research an IEP and keep notes about accommodation you provide while homeschooling.

7. **Ask for help when needed.** Whether extra help, note takers, or special software, keep written notes establishing a record of the individualized program you teach at home, including timing and location of tests, presentation of materials, or other techniques you have used to improve understanding.

8. **Search for colleges that provide help.** Attend a college fair, visit interesting colleges, and contact the college's academic support department. Ask about the success of

other learning disabled (LD) students in their program.

9. **Accentuate strengths and achievements.** Create comprehensive homeschool records that show your homeschool's academic rigor without mentioning adaptations. Include an activity list, with volunteer work and employment successes.

10. **Arrange accommodation in college.** Prepare a list of reasonable adaptive services that might be helpful and discuss those with the college the student will attend.

Learning to Grow as Adults

Jay Smith of Linfield College says:

> The advice that I'd give to your students, is to simply be proactive in their college search process. The students shouldn't be afraid to ask

> colleges if they offer support for students with learning disabilities, and what that support entails. We have high expectations of our students, but we also understand that we all learn in different ways.

Some colleges have an extremely supportive environment for children with learning disabilities. Redeemer Pacific College is a small Catholic college in Langley, BC, affiliated with Canada's premier Christian liberal arts university, Trinity Western University. Admissions Coordinator Jennifer Friesen says:

> All RPC students are able to use the services for students with disabilities offered through TWU, including access to the Learning Resource Centre and starting off their university career at TWU's Freshman Academy.
>
> The Learning Resource Centre offers services such as note taking,

> accommodated examinations, and provides material in alternate formats.
>
> Freshman Academy is a program for students who have not met the requirements for admission into university due to a low grade point average or missing academic courses.

Friesen says:

> Freshman Academy allows students to go through their classes in a small cohort with the support of their professors, a faculty Learning Coach, and their classmates. Once students have completed Freshman Academy they are able to directly enter their second year of university at Redeemer Pacific and Trinity Western.

When I attend college fairs, I notice how many colleges truly specialize in students with learning struggles. They want your students to attend and they are ready, willing, and able to teach them.

Afterword

Who is Lee Binz and What Can She Do for Me?

Number one best-selling homeschool author, Lee Binz is The HomeScholar. Her mission is "helping parents homeschool high school." Lee and her husband, Matt, homeschooled their two boys, Kevin and Alex, from elementary through high school.

Upon graduation, both boys received four-year, full tuition scholarships from their first choice university. This enables Lee to pursue her dream job—helping parents homeschool their children through high school.

On The HomeScholar website, you will find great products for creating homeschool transcripts and comprehensive records to help you amaze and impress colleges.

Find out why Andrew Pudewa, Founder of the Institute for Excellence in Writing says, "Lee Binz knows how to navigate this often confusing and frustrating labyrinth better than anyone."

You can find Lee online at:

HomeHighSchoolHelp.com

If this book has been helpful, could you please take a minute to write us a quick review on Amazon? Thank you!

Testimonials

It is soooo affirming!

You have taken an enormous amount of information and put it into bite-sized pieces so that the homeschooling parent can learn the information and process without becoming overwhelmed and frustrated—that goes for beginner homeschool high school parents and those of us who have been at it awhile. And you speak in the videos like a girlfriend who is going through all the same stuff with me! I feel myself saying, "YES!!! That was your experience too!" It is soooo affirming! ~Sally in Washington

----

I cannot recommend her services highly enough!

As these kids were going through their high school years, my homeschool mentor, Lee Binz, helped me realize that seeing their individuality and capitalizing on this as well as their strengths and passions was the ticket to helping each of them gain entry into their next chapter of life. I am so thankful for the instruction, solid support, and mentorship that the HomeScholar provided to me as I went through the process of ensuring that their high school years were college preparatory for each of them, as well as preparing unique and beautiful homeschool records for each as they sought college entry. Lee made a potentially overwhelming task totally do-able. I will never regret the last twenty or so years of watching three precious ones become adults.

Lee has a heart for homeschool moms trying to sort through all the confusing information out there, she's not judgmental about doing things "the one way", and has a gift for doing her homework regarding everything from obtaining scholarships to preparing transcripts that showcase your child's uniqueness for colleges.

I cannot recommend her services highly enough. She also has much information for moms of middle-schoolers regarding course planning as well as many other helps for that season of homeschooling. How nice it would have been to have had that input during my middle-schooling years! ~ Mary in North Carolina

For more information about my **Total Transcript Solution** and **Comprehensive Record Solution**, go to:

www.TotalTranscriptSolution.com
www.ComprehensiveRecordSolution.com

Also From The HomeScholar...

- The HomeScholar Guide to College Admission and Scholarships: Homeschool Secrets to Getting Ready, Getting In and Getting Paid (Book and Kindle Book)
- Setting the Records Straight—How to Craft Homeschool Transcripts and Course Descriptions for College Admission and Scholarships (Book and Kindle Book)
- TechnoLogic: How to Set Logical Technology Boundaries and Stop the Zombie Apocalypse
- Finding the Faith to Homeschool High School

- Parent Training Classes (Online Training)
- High School Solution (Comprehensive Training, Tools, Resources, and Support)
- College Launch Solution (Comprehensive Training, Tools, Resources, and Support)
- Total Transcript Solution (Online Training, Tools and Templates)
- Comprehensive Record Solution (Online Training, Tools and Templates)
- Gold Care Club (Comprehensive Online Support and Training)
- Silver Training Club (Online Training)

The HomeScholar Coffee Break Books Released or Coming Soon on Kindle and Paperback:

- Delight Directed Learning: Guiding Your Homeschooler Toward Passionate Learning

- Creating Transcripts for Your Unique Child: Help Your Homeschool Graduate Stand Out from the Crowd
- Beyond Academics: Preparation for College and for Life
- Planning High School Courses: Charting the Course Toward High School Graduation
- Graduate Your Homeschooler in Style: Make Your Homeschool Graduation Memorable
- Keys to High School Success: Get Your Homeschool High School Started Right!
- Getting the Most Out of Your Homeschool This Summer: Learning just for the Fun of it!
- Finding a College: A Homeschooler's Guide to Finding a Perfect Fit
- College Scholarships for High School Credit: Learn and Earn With This Two-for-One Strategy!

- College Admission Policies Demystified: Understanding Homeschool Requirements for Getting In
- A Higher Calling: Homeschooling High School for Harried Husbands (by Matt Binz, Mr. HomeScholar)
- Gifted Education Strategies for Every Child: Homeschool Secrets for Success
- College Application Essays: A Primer for Parents
- Creating Homeschool Balance: Find Harmony Between Type A and Type Zzz...
- Homeschooling the Holidays: Sanity Saving Strategies and Gift Giving Ideas
- Your Goals this Year: A Year by Year Guide to Homeschooling High School
- Making the Grades: A Grouch-Free Guide to Homeschool Grading
- High School Testing: Knowledge That Saves Money

- Getting the BIG Scholarships: Learn Expert Secrets for Winning College Cash!
- Easy English for Simple Homeschooling: How to Teach, Assess and Document High School English
- Scheduling—The Secret to Homeschool Sanity: Plan You Way Back to Mental Health
- Junior Year is the Key to High School Success: How to Unlock the Gate to Graduation and Beyond
- Upper Echelon Education: How to Gain Admission to Elite Universities
- How to Homeschool College: Save Time, Reduce Stress and Eliminate Debt
- Homeschool Curriculum That's Effective and Fun: Avoid the Crummy Curriculum Hall of Shame!

- Comprehensive Homeschool Records: Put Your Best Foot Forward to Win College Admission and Scholarships
- Options After High School: Steps to Success for College or Career
- How to Homeschool 9th and 10th Grades: Simple Steps for Starting Strong!
- Senior Year Step-by-Step: Simple Instructions for Busy Homeschool Parents
- How to Homeschool Independently: Do-it-Yourself Secrets to Rekindle the Love of Learning
- High School Math The Easy Way: Simple Strategies for Homeschool Parents in Over Their Heads
- Homeschooling Middle School with Powerful Purpose: How to Successfully Navigate 6th through 8th Grades

- Simple Science for Homeschooling High School: Because Teaching Science isn't Rocket Science!
- How to Be Your Child's Best College Coach: Strategies for Success Using Teens You'll Find Lying Around the House

Would you like to be notified when we offer the next *Coffee Break Books* for FREE during our Kindle promotion days? If so, leave your name and email below and we will send you a reminder.

HomeHighSchoolHelp.com/
freekindlebook

Visit my Amazon Author Page!
amazon.com/author/leebinz

Made in the USA
Middletown, DE
04 December 2020

26190518R00060